SPECIAL REPORTS

RAPE CULTURE
AND SEXUAL VIOLENCE

BY REBECCA RISSMAN

CONTENT CONSULTANT
STEPHANIE A. SMITH
PROFESSOR, DEPARTMENT OF ENGLISH
UNIVERSITY OF FLORIDA

Essential Library

An Imprint of Abdo Publishing | abdopublis

abdopublishing.com

Published by Abdo Publishing, a division of ABDO, PO Box 398166, Minneapolis,
Minnesota 55439. Copyright © 2018 by Abdo Consulting Group, Inc. International
copyrights reserved in all countries. No part of this book may be reproduced in
any form without written permission from the publisher. Essential Library™ is a
trademark and logo of Abdo Publishing.

Printed in the United States of America, North Mankato, Minnesota
092017
012018

**THIS BOOK CONTAINS
RECYCLED MATERIALS**

Cover Photo: STR/AFP/Getty Images
Interior Photos: Jason Cohn/Reuters/Newscom, 4–5; Michael D. McElwain/
Steubenville Herald-Star/AP Images, 7; Keith Srakocic/AP Images, 11; The Print
Collector/Print Collector/Hulton Archive/Getty Images, 14–15; Charles Wilson Peale,
17; AP Images, 22; Krista Kennell/Sipa Press/slutwalklosangeleskk.026/1106050558/
Newscom, 28–29; Rick Majewski/NurPhoto/Sipa USA/AP Images, 35; Markus
Schreiber/AP Images, 36; Shutterstock Images, 38–39, 76–77; Sam Simmonds/
Polaris/Newscom, 42; Jim Wells/AP Images, 45; Angelos Tzortzinis/AFP/Getty
Images, 46; Mark Elias/AP Images, 48–49; Bettmann/Getty Images, 53; John
Locher/AP Images, 55; Pat Sullivan/AP Images, 57; Gabriela Maj/Patrick McMullan/
Getty Images, 59; Betsy Blaney/AP Images, 62–63; Jeff Neira/Disney ABC
Television Group/Getty Images, 66; Paul Elias/AP Images, 71; Mary Altaffer/AP
Images, 74; J. Scott Applewhite/AP Images, 82; Steve Zak Photography/WireImage/
Getty Images, 84–85; Jaco Marais/Foto24/Gallo Images/Getty Images, 86–87; J. M.
Eddins Jr./MCT/Tribune News Service/Getty Images, 90; Matt Rourke/AP Images, 94;
MediaPunch/Rex Features/Shutterstock/AP Images, 96

Editor: Arnold Ringstad
Series Designer: Maggie Villaume

Publisher's Cataloging-in-Publication Data

Names: Rissman, Rebecca, author.
Title: Rape culture and sexual violence / by Rebecca Rissman.
Description: Minneapolis, Minnesota : Abdo Publishing, 2018. | Series: Special reports
    | Includes bibliographic references and index.
Identifiers: LCCN 2017946873 | ISBN 9781532113352 (lib.bdg.) | ISBN 9781532152238
    (ebook)
Subjects: LCSH: Rape--Juvenile literature. | Sexual harassment of women--
    Juvenile literature. | Women--Crimes against--Juvenile literature. | Rape in
    mass media--Juvenile literature.
Classification: DDC 362.883--dc23
LC record available at https://lccn.loc.gov/2017946873

CONTENTS

CHAPTER ONE

A SUMMER
PARTY IN OHIO

O n the night of August 11, 2012, a high school house party raged in Steubenville, Ohio. A crowd of approximately 50 teenagers came from nearby towns to drink, dance, and blow off steam. Several popular members of the Steubenville High School football team made an appearance at the party. Steubenville was a tight-knit community. It prized its athletes.

At around midnight, it became clear that one partygoer was severely drunk. She was a 16-year-old girl from a nearby West Virginia town. Eventually, the girl left the party with a group of standout football stars from Steubenville, including 16-year-olds Ma'lik Richmond and Trent Mays. Together, the group headed

Steubenville and one of its high schools found themselves at the center of national media attention following a rape in August 2012.

Steubenville High School
"ROLL RED ROLL"

I-CATCH DISPLAYS   1-877-287-0100

GIRLS BASKETBALL
VS. WEIRTON
THURS. HOME @ 6

to a second party. After arriving, the girl started to vomit. Soon, the boys loaded her into a car and took her to her friend's house.

During the drive, a series of events began that would tear the community of Steubenville apart. Mays put his fingers inside the girl's vagina. He also opened her shirt to expose her breasts. Another teen in the back seat filmed the encounter on his cell phone. When they arrived at the friend's house, the girl vomited more. Her speech was slurred. She passed in and out of consciousness. Witnesses report seeing Mays and Richmond lying near the girl, touching her groin. Some reported seeing them put their fingers inside her vagina. Mays was seen putting his penis in her mouth. As each of these events transpired, witnesses took photos and videos of the girl and texted them to friends.

The following morning, the girl woke up at the friend's house naked, with no idea of what had happened. Friends picked her up and brought her home. But the incident was far from over. As the sun rose on August 12, 2012, social media was alight with photos, videos, and text messages documenting the girl's night. Eventually, Mays texted the girl, telling her he had just been taking care of her. She responded: "It's on youtube. I'm not stupid. Stop texting me."[1] Ten days later, Mays and Richmond were arrested.

A criminal investigation revealed that many teens in the Steubenville community were aware of what had

Protests erupted in the months following the incident.

happened that night because of social media and texts. Some scolded the teens for their behavior. Others joked about it. Some people pointed fingers at the girl, claiming her behavior had made the football team look bad. Many blamed the girl for drinking too much. One teen even posted a 12-minute video joking about how drunk she was.

Rape is a word that is often used, yet it is difficult to define. In fact, it has different definitions across the country and around the world. In a general sense, *rape* is the term used to describe any type of sexual assault in which sexual intercourse or penetration occurs against the consent of one party. Penetration can mean different things. It can refer to a penis, fingers, or other objects being put into a vagina, anus, or mouth. Rape can be perpetrated by men or women. Both men and women can be raped.

Sexual assault is the term used to describe sexual contact that occurs without consent. Sexual assault includes rape, sexual touching, and being forced to perform a sexual act on another person. Both rape and the broader category of sexual assault are types of sexual violence.

THE WORLD REACTS

News of the event divided the community of Steubenville, and soon, the nation. Some thought the girl was at fault. They believed she was aware of what she was doing and simply became embarrassed after the fact. They accused the girl of tarnishing the reputations of the promising athletes. Many took the other side. They thought the girl had been raped. They believed Mays and Richmond were at fault. Still others were angry at another group: the bystanders. These people were outraged that a girl's violation had been so widely seen on social media without

UPDATING THE FBI'S DEFINITION

For decades, the Federal Bureau of Investigation (FBI) defined rape as an event involving "carnal knowledge of a female forcibly and against her will."[2] This language was problematic for several reasons. First, the term *carnal knowledge* implied that rape could occur only if a man had sexual intercourse with a woman. This left out other types of sexual violations. Second, this language suggested that only women could be the victims of rape. Finally, it implied that force had to be involved for a sexual act to be nonconsensual.

In 2013, the FBI changed its definition of rape. It is now defined as "penetration, no matter how slight, of the vagina or anus with any body part or object, or oral penetration by a sex organ of another person, without the consent of the victim."[3] Many have praised the FBI for adopting this new definition. They believe the more inclusive, gender neutral language will help victims seek legal recourse. They also believe it will result in punishment for more perpetrators of sexual violence.

ANONYMOUS AND STEUBENVILLE

A group of online activists, or hacktivists, believed the town of Steubenville was conspiring to downplay the rape and its aftermath. The activists decided to take action to draw attention to the case. Deric Lostutter, a 29-year-old hacker, worked with other hackers in the group Anonymous to target a Steubenville football website. They illegally gained access to the site and leaked personal information about people involved. As their actions went viral, they succeeded in getting the case more attention. Anonymous staged several protests.

However, not everyone celebrated the actions of these hacktivists. Many pointed to their criminal behavior. Their hacking had broken laws. Lostutter ultimately pleaded guilty to helping plot the actions against the website. He was sentenced to two years in federal prison.

more protest. Why, they asked, hadn't someone intervened to protect the girl?

Ultimately, Mays and Richmond were found guilty of rape in 2013. Mays was sentenced to a minimum of two years in a youth prison. Richmond was sentenced to a minimum of one year. The range of media responses showed that this controversy was far from resolved. Many media outlets reported the guilty verdict with a sense of satisfaction. CNN correspondent Poppy Harlow reacted with sympathy. She reported that it was "incredibly difficult, even for an outsider like me, to watch what happened as these two young men that had such promising futures, star football players, very good students, literally watched as they believed their lives fell apart."[4]

Some people in the media saw the Steubenville events as a prime example of something known as rape culture. This is the name for the setting in which rape and other types of sexual violence are normalized and common. In rape culture, specific behaviors and attributes are associated with each gender. Violent male sexuality is supported. Women's bodies are objectified. Male perpetrators of sexual violence are not seen as terrible criminals. Rather, their actions are excused as the result

Mays, *left*, and Richmond

GENDER LINES

The vast majority of sexual assaults and rapes are committed against women. Approximately 91 percent of victims of rape and sexual assault are female. However, that is not the end of the story. Approximately 9 percent of victims of rape and sexual assault are men.[6] Men in this group report having been penetrated, or having been forced to penetrate someone else against their will.

Most people think of rape as something that predominantly happens to women. But unwanted sexual contact is something that affects both genders. In 2012, a survey revealed that both men and women experienced a range of unwanted sexual contact in nearly identical numbers. When asked if they had experienced nonrape sexual violence in the last year, including unwanted noncontact sexual experiences, 1 in 20 men and women said yes.[7] Noncontact sexual experiences can include unwanted exposure to sexual images, being flirted with, or similar events.

of natural, typically harmless male urges. Excuses such as "boys will be boys" are common within rape culture. Victims in rape culture are often not listened to. Their complaints are dismissed, and their actions or appearance are often blamed for their assaults.

AN AMERICAN EPIDEMIC

Rape and other forms of sexual assault are a large problem in the United States. The statistics are staggering. Every 98 seconds, an American is sexually assaulted. An average of 321,500 people are victims of rape or sexual assault each year in the United States.[5] In 2015, President Barack Obama weighed in on the issue, saying, "Nearly one in five women in America has been a victim of rape or attempted rape. . . . It's not okay. And it has to stop."[8]

Some feel that rape culture is to blame for the American sexual violence epidemic. Others believe this is too simplistic. They argue that there are greater factors influencing the rates and reporting of sexual violence in America. Diving into this debate involves exploring the history of attitudes about sexual assault, gender roles, feminism, media, and politics.

"BLURRED LINES"

In March 2013, Robin Thicke released "Blurred Lines," a song about a woman in a nightclub who showed mixed signals toward the singer. The lyrics hinted that the singer would ignore a woman's refusal.

The album on which the song appeared debuted at number one on *Billboard*'s album chart. In its very first week, it sold 177,000 copies. However, within months of the song's release, various writers noted that its lyrics sounded similar to the words rapists used to coerce their victims.

The controversy surrounding the song only increased when 37-year-old Thicke took the stage with 20-year-old Miley Cyrus to perform it at the 2013 Video Music Awards. Critics noted that the age difference between the performers contributed to the unhealthy notions about consent perpetuated by the song. Many were offended. Thicke's career has struggled in the years following "Blurred Lines." Many attribute this to the public backlash that followed the song's release.

CHAPTER TWO

THE EVOLVING HISTORY OF RAPE CULTURE

Ancient attitudes about sexual violence reflected the low, powerless position most women held in society. Rapes were often thought of as the theft of a woman's virginity, rather than as an assault on her person. In many cultures, such as Ancient Rome, a woman's virginity was not something she was in charge of. It was thought of as property that belonged to the men in her family. Therefore, a rape was an affront to a woman's male relatives. In many cultures, victims of rape were even punished for their sexual impurity.

In Ancient Roman tradition, the rape of Lucretia, *right*, was a pivotal moment in the founding of the Roman Republic.

In Babylonia, for example, if a married woman were raped, she would be put to death for her "crime."

Not all historical cultures held these notions about rape. In some Middle Atlantic Native American tribes, such as the Iroquois, rape was a rare phenomenon that was very strictly punished. One English trader of the 1700s remarked that a man in this region might be "putt to Death for Committing Rapes, which is a Crime [the Native Americans there] Despise."[1]

AMERICAN RAPE

Cultural attitudes about rape have shifted throughout American history. The concept of human ownership played an important role in this evolution. Historically, women were often considered the property of the men in their lives. Wives belonged to their husbands. Within this social construct, rape was an action taken against property, not a person. This meant that marital rape was legal. This concept also applied to racial inequality in America. The institution of slavery, which relied on the notion that black people were property, led to widespread sexual violence

Historians believe Founding Father Thomas Jefferson was one of many slaveholders who fathered children with enslaved women—in this case, with his slave Sally Hemings.

against black people. Enslaved people were often raped by their owners or other white men.

The power dynamic created by the idea of human ownership affected the way rape was punished. In the country's early years, white women who were sexually assaulted had little ability to seek justice. In the rare instances in which a white woman chose to prosecute her rapist, white perpetrators often received minimal punishments. For example, in 1793, Lanah Sawyer was pulled into a New York City brothel and raped by a man she had been walking with. She took her case to court and listened as the defendant's lawyer claimed she had consented to the rape by agreeing to walk with the man. In the end, the man was acquitted.

The situation was very different for black people. Black men who were accused of raping white women were often punished much more severely than white men facing the same claims. In the South, white men were not punished for sexual crimes committed against slaves. In fact, the rape of slaves was not considered a crime at all.

Black people in the free North also suffered from sexual violence at the hands of whites. One example of this occurred in the early 1800s, when a black woman named Sylvia Patterson was raped by Captain James Dunn in New York City. Patterson took him to court. In the end, her attacker was not convicted of rape. Rather, he was simply fined $1. In the process, Patterson was accused of being promiscuous and of having a sexually transmitted infection.

Even after slavery was abolished following the end of the American Civil War (1861–1865), black Americans continued to struggle against sexual violence. In 1866, a 16-year-old black girl named Lucy Smith was raped by

MORE TO THE
STORY

ROSA PARKS

Rosa Parks, the black seamstress who in 1955 refused to move to the back of a segregated bus in Montgomery, Alabama, is famous for her work in the civil rights movement. But few today realize that some of her most important activism had nothing to do with bus seats. Instead, it had to do with rape.

In 1931, an 18-year-old Parks was nearly raped by a white neighbor. She recorded the experience in a letter: "He moved nearer to me and put his hand on my waist. . . . I was trapped and helpless. I was hurt and sickened through with anger and disgust."[2] Parks was not alone in this experience. Black women were often the victims of unwanted sexual contact. They often struggled to find justice. Law enforcement could be uncooperative, hostile, or even involved in the sexual assaults.

Black men experienced a different type of victimization. They were often wrongly accused of sexual violence toward white women. Parks met her husband, Raymond, in the 1930s, when he was raising funds for a group of black men who had been falsely accused of raping two white women. The issue of rape affected many parts of the black community. Parks wanted to do something about it.

Parks became the branch secretary of the Montgomery organization of the National Association for the Advancement of Colored People (NAACP). One of her duties was to find justice for black victims of sexual assault. She traveled to small Alabama towns to investigate incidents of sexual violence committed against black women. She encouraged black women to speak out about these injustices. And she brought their stories back to Montgomery, where activists used these accounts in protests and news stories.

seven white men, including two law enforcement officers. Smith testified against her attackers in court. None of the men were punished for their actions.

Black men also suffered from this racial power disparity, especially with regard to their interactions with white women. They could be harshly punished for any actions deemed sexually inappropriate. In North Carolina in 1950, for example, one black man was sentenced to two years of hard labor after he looked at a white teenage girl.

Sexual violence plagued many American women throughout the 1900s. As women began to emerge from the household to take on clerical jobs and manufacturing work, they were exposed to the verbal and physical assaults of male bosses, coworkers, and passersby. If the actions of a woman's male colleague became too aggressive, her only viable solution was often to quit her job.

The women's rights movement, which began in 1848, championed women's rights in many aspects of American life up through the early 1900s. Activists in this movement traveled the country to speak about the unfair treatment of women. One of the things they argued against was the way husbands had ownership of their wives and could

abuse them with few consequences. The movement also

focused on women's right to

work in the jobs they wanted

under safe conditions. The

activists fought for women's

right to vote, too. Eventually,

this movement contributed

to the suffrage movement.

When women gained the vote

across the country in 1920, this

achievement signified a shift in

American culture. Women who

could vote were recognized as

full citizens, not property.

In the 1960s and 1970s, the

second wave of the women's

rights movement formed.

This time, it was known as the

women's liberation movement.

Also known as the feminist movement, this was a social

and political movement that encouraged women to fight

RAPE CULTURE IN ADVERTISING

Media can often reflect cultural attitudes. Examining some vintage print advertisements shows how the awareness of rape culture has changed over time. One advertisement from the 1960s shows a crowd of trouser-clad men grabbing at a woman dressed in only her underwear. The line under the photo reads, "Ring around Rose. Or Carol. Or Eleanor, etc. But you can only play if you wear Broomstick slacks."[3] The ad seems playful. The men are clearly smiling. However, the woman's face is hard to see. Modern critics have pointed to ads like this to argue that rape culture was much more accepted in the past. They suggest that the imagery and language in this ad promote the idea of multiple men taking advantage of one woman. And the smiles and lighthearted language minimize the danger of the situation.

The women's liberation movement brought new attention to sexism in society.

male oppression and promote the rights of women. A large component of the women's liberation movement involved encouraging women to speak out about their own experiences with sexual assault.

In 1975, several important events changed the way people thought about sexual violence. First, the term *sexual harassment* was coined. This is the name for any unwanted verbal or physical sexual advances. Second, feminist author Susan Brownmiller published a book called *Against Our Will: Men, Women, and Rape*. It helped to bring rape into the headlines, and it also inspired women to think of rape as something that contributed to the dominance of men over women. Brownmiller highlighted the sexual violence that often occurs within marriages, in relationships, or even between casual acquaintances. She warned readers: "The typical American rapist might be the boy next door."[4] Finally, 1975 also saw the release of a documentary film called *Rape Culture*, which introduced many to this term and concept. The film sought to raise awareness of the prominence and acceptance of sexual violence. It showed how magazines, music, and film all contributed to the idea that rape was normal and unavoidable.

RAPE CULTURE'S EVOLUTION

In the 1970s, most of the thinking about rape culture had to do with the way men treated women. Many feminists believed that sex work, such

RAPE CULTURE IN MUSIC

Today, many people criticize musicians for perpetuating ideas about sexual violence in their lyrics and imagery. For example, when Kanye West and Katy Perry collaborated on the song "ET," the following lines raised eyebrows:

First I'ma disrobe you,
then I'ma probe you,
see I abducted you,
so I tell you what to do

This phenomenon is not new. In fact, some of America's classic songs feature lyrics that could be interpreted as promoting rape culture. In the famed 1944 song "Baby, It's Cold Outside," a woman sings lines such as "I simply must go" and "The answer is no," while a man pressures her otherwise with lines like "What's the sense in hurting my pride?" and "Oh baby, don't hold out."

as prostitution, contributed to rape culture. They also believed that pornography was part of the problem. They pointed to these as contributing factors in the way rape was normalized and even encouraged.

As more people learned about rape and rape culture, some activists looked for new ways to prevent sexual assault. They also worked to help victims of sexual assault heal from their traumas and prosecute their attackers. In 1972, the first rape crisis centers opened. These early centers were often organized by fellow rape survivors and focused on giving women a space to talk about their experiences. Over time, these centers evolved to include self-defense classes, to host marches to raise awareness of rape, and to encourage anti-rape education at colleges and universities.

In the mid-1970s, anti-rape activists started the Take Back

MINORS AND RAPE

Sexual abuse of children by adults is not typically included in discussion of rape culture. However, it is still a pervasive American problem. Estimates are hard to come by because children often do not report their abuse, but one study found that 1 in 5 girls and 1 in 20 boys is the victim of child sexual abuse.[5] Another phenomenon, statutory rape, involves an adult having sex with a minor. Minors are considered unable to consent to sexual activity. The age of consent differs across states, ranging from 16 to 18.

the Night movement. They marched through city streets at night, holding candles. These marches served two purposes. They honored the victims of sexual violence and also protested against that violence. These marches soon spread. Today, Take Back the Night marches happen each year across the country.

Over time, many people came to think about rape culture differently. This term now includes the experiences of male victims and acknowledges that women can be perpetrators of sexual violence. It also highlights the experiences faced by minorities, transgender people, and lesbian and gay people.

ARGUING AGAINST THE NOTION OF RAPE CULTURE

Not everyone agrees that rape culture exists. *Time* magazine writer Caroline Kitchens wrote that while "rape is certainly a serious problem, there's no evidence that it's considered a cultural norm."[6] Others have simply found fault with the concept of rape culture. Conservative columnist Barbara Kay acknowledges that rape is a problem but argues that it is not the pandemic suggested

THE LGBTQ COMMUNITY

People who identify as lesbian, gay, bisexual, transgender, or queer (LGBTQ) often experience sexual violence at higher rates than heterosexuals. The high incidence of sexual violence in this community likely has several causes. LGBTQ people often encounter higher rates of poor treatment, stigma, poverty, or exclusion from their peers. Experts have found that these factors put people at a higher risk for sexual violence. LGBTQ people are also often the target of hate crimes. Sometimes, hate crimes involve sexual assaults.

A look at the numbers reveals that some forms of sexual violence are often more common in the LGBTQ community. About 13 percent of lesbian women and 17 percent of heterosexual women have been raped. However, 46 percent of bisexual women have been raped. Approximately 40 percent of gay men and 47 percent of bisexual men have experienced non-rape sexual assault. These numbers are much higher than the rate at which heterosexual men experience non-rape sexual assault: 21 percent.[8]

by the phrase *rape culture*. She writes, "To result in a *culture*, a phenomenon must be widely accepted as the *norm*."[7] For Kay and some others, this isn't the case with rape.

Some feel that the focus on rape culture takes away from the attention that should be paid to perpetrators of sexual violence. The Rape, Abuse & Incest National Network (RAINN) is the largest anti–sexual violence organization in the United States. It encourages society to shift its focus from rape culture to the individuals engaging in sexual assault and rape. In a 2014 letter to the White House, the president and vice president of RAINN stressed that "rape is not caused by cultural factors but by the conscious decisions of a small percentage of the community to commit a violent crime."

Kitchens points out another problem with blaming rape culture for all rape. She says that "by blaming so-called rape culture, we implicate all men in a social atrocity . . . and deflect blame from the rapists truly responsible for sexual violence."[9]

Kitchens has also questioned the truth behind the existence of a rape culture on college campuses. In 2013, she wrote an article in *US News & World Report* that pointed out the inconsistencies in the way rape data was collected. She pointed to a Department of Justice survey that suggested that only 1 in every 40 college students was raped. This ratio was much lower than the one-in-five ratio frequently reported. Kitchens suggested that rape culture was not real but was instead the result of "inflated statistics and alarmist depictions of campus culture."[10]

CHAPTER THREE

SLUT SHAMING AND VICTIM BLAMING

The word *slut* has a long and complex history. It has been used to describe men and women. In the past it was used to talk about people who were dirty, lazy, and sexually promiscuous. In Geoffrey Chaucer's *Canterbury Tales,* written in the 1300s, a character uses the word when discussing a sloppy-looking man.

Today, there are still different meanings and connotations for the word *slut*. In some circles, the word has a sex-positive meaning. In progressive or feminist

Activists have mobilized in response to the idea that women who are raped have brought it on themselves by the way they dress or behave.

groups, it can describe people who take ownership of and pride in their autonomy to make sexual decisions.

However, the majority of people use the word to mean something else. Most use *slut* to describe a woman who is sexually active or does not conform to cultural expectations of how a woman should act. Women can be called sluts for acting, dressing, speaking, or otherwise behaving in a manner deemed sexually provocative.

This definition is fluid. Individuals interpret behavior in different ways. What one person considers to be normal behavior could be considered provocative by another.

Slut shaming is the name for the practice of shaming a woman for being sexually active or appearing to be sexually active. Slut shaming is also often directed at women who appear to enjoy sexual activity.

"I DON'T THINK THAT WE SHOULD BE TELLING WOMEN ANYTHING. I THINK WE SHOULD BE TELLING MEN NOT TO RAPE WOMEN AND START THE CONVERSATION THERE. YOU'RE TALKING ABOUT THIS AS IF IT'S SOME FACELESS, NAMELESS CRIMINAL, WHEN A LOT OF TIMES IT'S SOMEONE YOU KNOW AND TRUST. . . . IF YOU TRAIN MEN NOT TO GROW UP TO BECOME RAPISTS, YOU PREVENT RAPE."[1]

—ZERLINA MAXWELL, POLITICAL COMMENTATOR ON FOX NEWS'S *HANNITY*

A VICIOUS CYCLE

Women who are labeled sluts are often targeted for sexual assault. After they have been sexually assaulted, many victims are retrospectively labeled as sluts. Some victims are reluctant to report their sexual assaults for fear of being called sluts. This vicious cycle makes slut shaming especially troubling.

In the 2004 movie *Mean Girls,* actress Tina Fey's character lectures a crowd of teenage girls: "You've got to stop calling each other sluts and whores. It just makes it okay for guys to call you sluts and whores."[2] The character's comments refer to the fact that both men and women use pejorative words to describe sexually active women. A 2014 study

VICTIM SUICIDES

People who are the targets of slut shaming can experience dangerous psychological trauma. Being slut shamed can cause embarrassment, shame, and feelings of helplessness. Social media has made this problem even worse. Photos and stories of sexual assault that are shared on social media can reach huge numbers of people very quickly. This can make victims feel even more violated.

In 2012, a 15-year-old California girl was raped while unconscious at a party. A revealing photo of her assault was passed around on social media. The victim was so ashamed that she killed herself after posting one last message on her Facebook wall: "The whole school knows . . . my life is ruined. . . . I have a reputation I can never get rid of."[3]

Rape victims are 13 times more likely to attempt suicide than nonvictims. Rape victims who experience slut shaming must struggle to deal not only with their assault but also with the social fallout that often accompanies it.

ANTI-RAPE PRODUCTS

Today, new products are flooding the marketplace to help prevent sexual assaults. One of these products is Undercover Colors, a nail polish that changes colors when it comes into contact with date rape drugs. *Date rape* is the term used to describe a sexual assault that is perpetrated by someone the victim knows. It often happens after a date or friendly encounter. Date rape drugs are substances that can incapacitate a victim, making him or her more vulnerable to an unwanted sexual advance. A common date rape drug is Rohypnol, often called "roofies." Undercover Colors allows women to dip their painted nails into a drink and test the liquid for drugs. If a date rape drug is present in the drink, their nail polish will change colors, thus alerting them to danger.

Some have applauded products like Undercover Colors. They claim that they put power back into the hands of women to prevent their own assaults. Others have pointed to Undercover Colors as promoting the notion that it is a woman's duty to stop herself from being raped. They argue that it is first and foremost the attacker's responsibility to control his or her own behavior.

performed by the think tank Demos confirmed this. It showed that women tweet the word *slut* nearly as often as men.

SLUT SHAMING AND RAPE CULTURE

While the word *slut* can be used to describe men, it is almost always used for women. This double standard, in which women are assigned a negative word for sexual identities and men are not, is a crucial component in the concept of rape culture.

In rape culture, male sexuality is natural and normal, even when it manifests itself violently. Female sexuality, on the other hand, is thought of as abnormal. Cultural pressures on women may suggest they should dress, act, and speak in ways that are inviting to men, yet they must never cross an invisible line that separates their "sexy" behaviors from "slutty" ones. Within rape culture, women who pursue sexual encounters are inappropriate, and a woman who acts sexually is inviting her own assault.

Slut shaming is often pointed to within discussions of rape culture as a way to minimize a sexual assault by suggesting that the victim was clearly interested in sexual activity because of her behavior. Emily Lindin, the founder of the UnSlut Project, commented on this phenomenon:

> One of the easiest ways for the media or the public to dismiss a woman's report of sexual assault is to claim that she is a slut. We make it a priority to investigate her prior, consensual sexual history, dragging up old rumors, photos, and relationships to demonstrate that she is a promiscuous, lewd woman. One who couldn't possibly have been raped. It's as if proving that she gave consent once, to something, proves that she no longer has the right to refuse consent. To anything.[4]

Some wonder if confronting slut shaming might help people become aware of rape culture. Others think it is yet another example of misdirected focus. They argue

SLUTWALKS

SlutWalks are protest events in which people gather together to call for an end to rape culture and raise awareness of the harms of slut shaming. SlutWalks often specifically protest the way some rape victims are blamed for their own assaults because of what they were wearing.

Many SlutWalk participants dress as "sluts," wearing provocative clothing or even just underwear. Some use markers or paint to physically label their bodies with words like "slut" or "whore." They do this both to raise awareness of the way these words are used, and also to reclaim the words themselves.

Some object to SlutWalks, saying they do more harm than good. They argue that a group of women marching in their underwear does not send a message of female empowerment, instead simply providing a show for men who are watching.

that discussion about slut shaming takes the public's attention away from the real problem: rapists.

WHEN A VICTIM IS "ASKING FOR IT"

Similar to slut shaming, *victim blaming* is the name for casting some or even all of the responsibility for an assault on the victim rather than the perpetrator. Victim blaming can take many forms. When, for example, a woman is raped after a night of drinking, many point to her drunkenness as a contributing factor in her assault. Victims who were walking in an unsafe area or accepting a ride from a stranger are often painted by the media, law enforcement, or even friends as having acted in a way that invited their assault.

At events called SlutWalks, activists work to bring an end to the practice of slut shaming.

Victim blaming remains a controversial issue. Some

people believe that potential victims of sexual assault

should be educated about high-risk behaviors, such as

Protest events calling attention to issues of victim blaming have sprung up around the world.

drug or alcohol abuse or going home with people they don't know. They argue that if a victim has engaged in behaviors that put her in danger, then she is at least partially responsible for the outcome.

Others disagree. They think that regardless of a person's behavior, that person should not be at risk for sexual violence. They believe that all attention should focus on the attacker. They argue that focusing on a victim's inebriation, dress, or behavior reinforces rape culture, in which rape is so common that potential victims must be diligent about avoiding it.

DERRICK ROSE

In 2015, the former girlfriend of NBA player Derrick Rose accused him and two friends of gang-raping her while she was unconscious. During the subsequent trial, Rose's legal team repeatedly used tactics that some felt slut shamed the woman. For example, his defense argued that she used social media to "portra[y] herself as sexual," citing Instagram photos in which she is "dressed in provocative attire, is in sexually suggestive poses, and is in photographs indicating that she engages in sexually charged encounters with more than one man at a time."[5]

The judge quickly ruled that he would not allow victim-blaming rhetoric in court, commenting, "Defendant Rose appears to suggest that women who publicly portray themselves as 'sexual' are less likely to experience embarrassment, humiliation, and harassment associated with gang rape. Such rhetoric has no place in this court."[6] In the end, the three men were acquitted of the charges.

CHAPTER FOUR

THE MASCULINE
IDEAL

Powerful. Rugged. In control. Tough. Physical. Muscular. These are words and phrases typically associated with men. They come from a masculine ideal created by movies, books, television, professional athletes, and other sources. The words sometimes associated with women are different: weak, quiet, passive, and pretty.

Of course, humans are complex and unique. Every woman and every man is different. A man might embody a few traits associated with masculinity and a few traits associated with femininity. And that same man may also embody traits not associated with either gender.

Notions of masculinity and femininity are deeply tied to the idea of rape culture.

MASCULINITIES STUDIES

Today, colleges and universities around the world feature women's studies classes and departments. One professor at Stony Brook University in New York is pioneering the first masculinities studies program. Dr. Michael Kimmel started the program to teach students to think critically about the many ways to be a man. He integrates different disciplines in his program, such as social work, health, and literature. He encourages his students to think about how race, sexuality, and pop culture have all impacted the masculine ideals. He wonders if having a better understanding of men could help reduce crimes such as rape.

Some common phrases contribute to this gender divide. Young boys are often told to "man up" when they are hurt or scared. This tells them to be less emotional and more physical. It tells them to be less unique and show more of the stereotypical male traits idealized in society. Often, when males behave poorly, their actions are excused with the phrase "boys will be boys." This simple phrase troubles some people. They argue that it explains away bad male behavior as natural and unavoidable. These common phrases add up to describe a version of masculinity that is fundamentally tough and destructive. This becomes especially problematic when applied to sexual activity. If men are born to be tough and destructive, then sexual violence could also be an unavoidable development.

DONALD TRUMP AND THE *ACCESS HOLLYWOOD* TAPE

In 2016, a video surfaced that showed then-presidential candidate Donald Trump and television host Billy Bush preparing to film an episode of *Access Hollywood*. Perhaps unaware that he was wearing a microphone, Trump spoke with Bush while inside a studio bus. His microphone picked up a conversation about how Trump seduces women: "I just start kissing them. It's like a magnet. Just kiss. I don't even wait. And when you're a star, they let you do it. You can do anything. Grab them by the p****. You can do anything."[1]

SOLDIERS AND VIOLENT SEXUALITY

The US military has a sexual assault problem. In 2013, the Department of Defense released a report that estimated approximately 26,000 service members experienced "unwanted sexual contact." In that same year, only 3,374 incidents were actually reported. Military victims of sexual assault are often hesitant to report their attackers for fear of disrupting camaraderie or looking bad to their peers. The military has also relied on a chain of command to handle matters such as rape. This means a victim must first report the incident to his or her commanding officer, who then passes the report up the line. If a victim is abused by a commanding officer, he or she is unlikely to report the assault.

One woman who was raped by a superior officer while in Iraq tried to report her assault multiple times. Each time she was blocked or discouraged. Today she is still angry that her attacker went unpunished: "He is free and able to do it again as long as he wears the uniform. The uniform represents a protective shield if you're a rapist with rank."[2]

41

Protesters quickly responded to the tape of Trump on *Access Hollywood.*

Many found this conversation troubling. Some said Trump was describing inappropriate sexual behavior. Civil rights lawyer Lisa Bloom believed the video described more than that: "Let's be very clear, he is talking about sexual assault. He is talking about grabbing a woman's genitals without her consent."[3]

Trump apologized for the video. He explained that his comments were just "locker-room banter." Some accepted his apology. Former vice presidential candidate Sarah Palin acknowledged that Bush's and Trump's comments were "disgusting," but reminded the public that "both boys apologized for them."[4] Others hesitated to pardon Trump and Bush for their conversation. They argued that the "locker-room banter" excuse was just another version of "boys will be boys," a phrase that allows men to behave poorly because of their gender. Using the word *boys* rather than *men* suggests that the people involved are not expected to take personal responsibility for their actions as adults.

VIOLENT MASCULINITY

Some experts have pointed to a troubling association between masculinity and sexual violence. They note that idealized traits such as toughness and power can quickly become sexual aggression. In war zones, this can be seen when an army invades a town and then rapes the women. This has occurred throughout history, but has most recently happened in Sudan, Guatemala, and the Democratic Republic of the Congo. The violence of war quickly bleeds into sexual violence.

Violent masculine sexuality doesn't just happen in war. Masculinity often merges with violent sexuality in movies when an action hero pulls a woman in for a kiss after saving the day. The viewer assumes the woman is interested in the kiss, but did the hero pause to get her consent? And what about any actions that follow the kiss? Stolen kisses on film may encourage similar actions in real life.

Some experts note that sexual violence is not about sex at all. Rather, they insist, it is a manifestation of masculine power. Writer Gloria Steinem and journalist Lauren Wolfe described this phenomenon: "Neither in war zones nor in street gangs is rape primarily about sex. It is sexualized violence whose motive is power, control, and proving a false image of manhood."[5] This image of manhood is central to rape culture.

FOOTBALL AND MASCULINITY

Football players are beloved American heroes. They are also a good example of the violent masculinity that troubles some critics. Professional football players are seen as muscular, tough, and wealthy men who spend their careers inflicting referee-sanctioned violence on one another. In contrast, slim cheerleaders wearing revealing uniforms bounce and smile for the crowds, often earning a tiny fraction of the salary enjoyed by football players. While individual football players are lauded for their talent and aggression, the nameless cheerleaders are appreciated for their bodies. Football games have nothing to do with rape. But many people point to the gender dynamics on display during football games as emblematic of the problems within rape culture.

REDEFINING MANHOOD

Many groups are working to redefine masculinity to embody a more peaceful, less violent ideal. Groups

Steinem has been a leading women's rights activist for decades.

such as A Call to Men educate men about violence against women, sexual assault, harassment, and bullying. The National Organization for Men against Sexism is an activist organization that works to promote a pro-feminist, LGBTQ, anti-racist perspective for young men.

Redefining manhood is one way some people are choosing to confront the idea of rape culture. They hope that by assigning new characteristics to manliness, such as kindness and patience, they might reduce the prevalence of sexual violence.

THE MASCULINE IDEAL IN THE GAY COMMUNITY

Within the gay community, some gay men identify as more masculine or feminine than others. Gay men who identify as masculine are often idealized, whereas those who are more feminine are looked down upon. Scott Rheinheimer, the University of Virginia LGBTQ Center Director, says, "A lot of times masculinity is still a coveted role for a partner in any type of intimacy." He added that sometimes, the "feminine role is still vilified or ostracized."[6]

Scientists have found that within gay circles, some men feel pressured to live up to an image of masculinity. This can result in sexual violence. Gay men living with a partner in a romantic relationship experience sexual assault at higher rates than their heterosexual peers. About 15 percent of gay men reported being raped, stalked, or otherwise sexually assaulted by their domestic partners.[7]

Many men have joined with women in condemning sexism in society.

CHAPTER FIVE

FALSE
REPORTING

O n a July night in 1977, a 16-year-old girl in a
Chicago suburb told police she had been raped.
When the officers showed her a photo lineup,
she pointed to an image of Gary Dotson, then age 24.
Dotson was arrested, charged with rape, and sentenced
to up to 50 years in prison.

However, the rape had never occurred. The girl later
admitted that she had made it up. She was trying to
cover for the possibility that her boyfriend may have
gotten her pregnant, which did not end up happening.
In 1985, racked with guilt, she retracted her previous
claims. Eventually, DNA evidence exonerated Dotson
in 1989.

Dotson spoke to the media following his exoneration.

Stories about false rape reports often captivate the media. Reporters jump at the chance to narrate the twisted plots that lead people to accuse one another of invented crimes. Though these stories can often dominate the headlines, they are actually very rare.

Experts estimate that only 2 to 10 percent of rape reports are fabricated.[1] This is similar to the rate at which other crimes, such as car thefts, are falsely reported. However, the public perception is that the number of false rape reports is much higher. In fact, one of the most commonly expressed reasons women do not report their rapes is that they fear they will not be believed.

REVENGE ACCUSATIONS

In the popular novel and film *Gone Girl*, the protagonist Amy falsely accuses a man of rape to get revenge on him after he tries to break up with her. The idea of women claiming rape to exact revenge is not new. While false rape accusations remain very rare, one of the most common motives for lying about being raped is revenge. The other two common motives are needing an alibi and wanting sympathy.

FALSE REPORTS AND RAPE CULTURE

False rape reports are a troubling component of rape culture. First, they are harmful to the accused. People who have been accused of rape must endure legal and emotional

50

strain as they hope to clear their own names. False rape reports are also harmful to people who have been victims of sexual assault in the past, or who may become victims in the future. Every time someone falsely claims to have been raped, it hurts the credibility of those who actually have been. Many experts claim that victims who believe false reporting is a common phenomenon may be less likely to report their own assaults. Victims might worry that they won't be believed, or that they will face harsh questioning in order to verify their claims.

Sometimes, false rape reports involve harmful racial stereotypes. Historically, black Americans have been portrayed as dangerous to whites. Black men especially were painted

GUILTY UNTIL PROVEN INNOCENT

Though they are statistically very rare, the men who are falsely accused of rape often suffer greatly. Police investigations and harsh treatment from their communities are often very challenging. Jay Cheshire was 17 years old when he was accused of rape. Though the allegations were withdrawn within weeks, the strain was too much on Cheshire. He killed himself two weeks after being acquitted.

One man who was falsely accused of rape created a website for victims of false accusations to share their stories and support one another. This man says he believes rape allegations should be taken seriously, but that he also wants to protect the wrongly accused: "Don't get me wrong, I absolutely have sympathy for a system that encourages complainants of rape to come forward. But, on the other hand, we now have a system that can be seen as open season for those who want to make false allegations of a sexual nature."[2]

as sexual predators of white women. These stereotypes were false and based on racist ideas. Some types of legal restrictions were created in part to minimize the dangers black sexuality supposedly posed for white women. Jim Crow laws, for example, enforced the separation of black and white people in the American South. They dictated that black people use only the facilities designated "colored." These laws were very serious. Black people who violated Jim Crow restrictions could be severely punished. If a black man was thought to have engaged in inappropriate behavior with a white woman, he may have been hanged, or lynched, in public. In 1954, the Supreme Court decision in *Brown v. Board of Education* determined that separate public schools for black and white students were unconstitutional. The following year, the Supreme Court ordered all states to integrate. This led to the dissolution of Jim Crow laws. Despite this, these laws and the racist attitudes behind them have had a lingering impact in modern culture. In 2017, a white woman claimed that she had been abducted and raped by three black men wearing ski masks. Though she later confessed to falsifying

A group of young African Americans, known in the media as the Scottsboro Boys, were falsely accused of rape in Alabama in 1931.

her report, many felt that her actions hurt not only rape survivors but also the African-American community.

Despite the rarity of false rape reporting, victims are often accused of lying about being sexually assaulted. This plays into the rape-culture phenomenon of victim blaming. Victims are portrayed as seeking attention for themselves. Sometimes they are accused of simply regretting their decisions and sexual behaviors and deciding to claim rape rather than face the consequences of their actions. These dismissals reinforce the notion that victims, especially women, are unreliable and not to be trusted. Men are seen as being in control and powerful.

FROM THE
HEADLINES

DONALD TRUMP ACCUSES HIS ACCUSERS

In 2016, more than ten women publicly accused then-presidential candidate Donald Trump of past sexual misconduct, such as kissing or groping without consent. Trump denied the allegations. He said that the claims were probably part of a smear campaign orchestrated by Hillary Clinton and the Democratic Party. Trump went on to threaten legal action against his accusers: "Every woman lied when they came forward to hurt my campaign. . . . The events never happened. Never. All of these liars will be sued after the election is over."[3]

Summer Zervos was one of the women who accused Trump of sexual assault. In January 2017, she sued Trump for defamation. The lawsuit claimed that Trump "used his national and international bully pulpit to make false factual statements to denigrate and verbally attack Ms. Zervos and the other women who publicly reported his sexual assaults."[4]

Trump went on to be elected president
following the allegations of sexual misconduct.

PROVING RAPE OCCURRED

Rape is an especially complicated crime to prove. Physical evidence, such as bodily fluids or clothing fibers, can be hard to collect. Witnesses to rape are rare. Alcohol or drugs, if consumed, can impair someone's memory. Often, authorities must struggle to determine which story—the accuser's or the accused's—to believe. If police officers handling the case are biased for or against the accuser, the officers' decisions might be skewed. Other times, a victim may decide to abandon a legal case against an attacker. Pursuing legal justice can be a long and drawn-out process, and some victims may find it to be a difficult ordeal.

These factors contribute to the idea that false rape reports are common. If a rape cannot be proved, or if

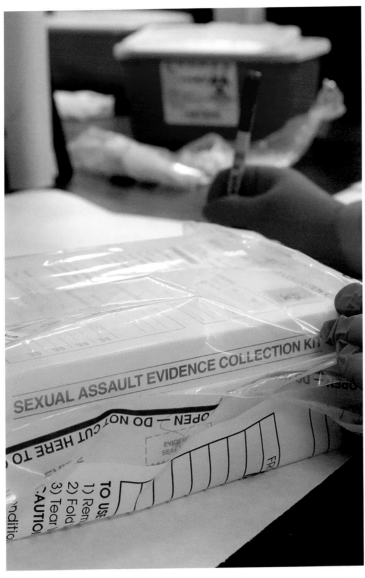

Medical professionals collect physical evidence from victims of rape. The evidence may later be used in a legal case.

an accuser decides not to pursue legal action against an attacker, some may think the attack was falsified. This is not necessarily the case.

MOVING FORWARD

As activists push to shed light on the rarity of false rape accusations, some suggest they are creating another problem by promoting the idea that women never lie.

WHEN VICTIMS DROP THE CHARGES

Some accusers end up recanting their statements to law enforcement. This means that they take back their statements. This can happen for several reasons. Some women feel pressured to do so by law enforcement. Others are intimidated by the legal process and choose to abandon it.

Sometimes rape cases are settled financially. For this to happen, the prosecution must drop its criminal case against the defendant. Then a civil case may follow in which the defendant can be sued for financial damages. In 2003, for example, a 20-year-old woman accused NBA player Kobe Bryant of raping her. She soon dropped her criminal charges against him. Later, both parties agreed to an out-of-court financial settlement of a civil lawsuit.

Feminist writer Catharine MacKinnon wrote in 1987 that feminism is "built on believing women's accounts of use and abuse by men."[5] At the time, this statement was daring in that it challenged society to listen to and accept stories of sexual abuse. Today, statements like these might encourage a blind acceptance of a woman's story, regardless of the details or truth of it.

Finding the delicate balance between the rights of the accuser and those of the accused is something

Catharine MacKinnon is a legal scholar who has focused on issues of sexual harassment and pornography.

MORE TO THE
STORY

THE DUKE LACROSSE TEAM

In 2006, members of the Duke University lacrosse team hosted a party. They paid two strippers to perform. Crystal Mangum, one of the strippers, later claimed that three players raped her during the party. Mangum is black. The three men she accused are white.

The three men were charged with rape. Duke suspended the lacrosse team from playing two games and then canceled the remainder of the season. The lacrosse coach was forced to resign. A lengthy court case followed, captivating the media. What came next shocked the world.

Investigators swabbed Mangum's vagina to test for DNA. These tests showed that there was no match to any of the accused lacrosse players. This alone did not discount Mangum's story. Experts say that the majority of rape prosecutions do not rely on DNA evidence. However, Mangum's lawyer withheld this DNA evidence from the prosecution. This made it seem as though he was acting dishonestly. He later left the case. Mangum was assigned a different lawyer. Then, her story began to change. She had trouble recalling the details of the alleged attack. In the end, the charges against the lacrosse players were dropped. The North Carolina attorney general even declared the players innocent. Despite this, Mangum continues to assert that she was assaulted.

people continue to struggle with today. Experts must learn to investigate a victim's claims in a way that does not alienate, blame, or revictimize through emotional turmoil. They must also keep the rights of the accused in mind, remembering that the accused are innocent until proven guilty. *Slate* writer Cathy Young urges her readers to remember both parties involved in a rape accusation: "Seeking justice for female victims should make us more sensitive, not less, to justice for unfairly accused men."[6]

CHAPTER SIX

THE COLLEGE
CAMPUS

In 2010, a fraternity at Yale University marched through campus chanting, "No means yes! Yes means anal!"[1] This chant joked not only about sex but also about consent. The Yale administration denounced these actions, and the fraternity was promptly kicked off campus for five years. Many wondered if enough had been done to punish the offenders. They wanted to extinguish the idea that consent was a joke. Just four years later, a fraternity at Texas Tech University hung a banner with the same message during a party.

At the beginning of the 2016 school year, parents arrived at Ohio University to drop off their freshman children. It was a happy and emotional time for many.

College campuses have become centers of controversy and debate related to rape culture.

One fraternity welcomed the new students with a series of banners hanging from its house. They were in clear view of the newly arriving students. One banner featured a scrawled message saying, "You taught morals, we'll teach her oral."[2] These banners may have been created as a joke, but many who witnessed them felt intimidated or offended.

A COLLEGE EPIDEMIC

Colleges and universities are experiencing a sexual assault epidemic. One study found that nearly 20 percent of female first-year students experienced rape or attempted rape during their freshman year. Some experts worry that this number may be misleading. Many college victims of sexual assault do not report their experiences to authorities. This means that the number of actual sexual assaults in college could be much higher.

Many factors contribute to the high rates of sexual assaults in college. New college students are often separated from their families and social circles for the first time. College students must make new friends, study new subjects, and navigate the world of adulthood on their own. In addition, they often abuse drugs and alcohol. The combination of these factors can lead some students to engage in high-risk behaviors, such as binge drinking, without a trusted social safety net to look out for them. Experts have even come to nickname the first few months of a freshman's college career the "red zone," since her risk for sexual assault during this time is so elevated.

RAPE AND THE GREEK SYSTEM

One segment of college students experiences sexual assault at an extremely high rate: those in the Greek fraternity and sorority system. Women in sororities are 74 percent more likely to be raped than their non-sorority peers. Men in fraternities are 300 percent more likely to commit rape than their non-fraternity peers.[3]

In 2016, ABC News broadcast a special program about questions of rape and consent on college campuses.

Some experts have hypothesized that these populations have such high rates of sexual assault because of the group attitudes of their members. Fraternities are male dominated and often encourage strong bonds of brotherhood. These bonds can extend to protecting one another's reputations, allowing poor behavior, and even covering up for one another. Fraternities are also often very socially powerful. They host the parties, they provide the alcohol, and they even dictate who may attend. This puts them in a position of power. The party guests are at their mercy. Since sororities are generally not allowed to serve alcohol, sorority girls often attend fraternity parties. Some feel that this unequal power dynamic combined with alcohol can lead to a high incidence of sexual assault.

Schools often report sexual assault statistics in different ways. This can make it seem as though different schools have vastly differing rates of sexual assault. Some of this can be attributed to school cultures, but most is explained by looking at the way schools categorize, handle, and encourage reports of sexual assault. Schools that report high rates of sexual assault may have reached these numbers by cultivating an environment in which students feel comfortable reporting sexual assault. Or these schools may report sexual assaults that have occurred between students but off campus. For example, during 2014, no rapes were reported on campus at New York University. However, six rapes were reported in off-campus properties that were linked to the school.

DISCIPLINE

College students who are victims of sexual violence may choose to report their assault to the police, to their school, or not at all. Many choose to report the incident to their school instead of the police. There are many reasons for this. Sometimes, student victims are not sure what constitutes a crime, and they feel as though their own

DATE RAPE DRUGS

Though people may think of rape as something that happens between two strangers in a dark alley, rape is often committed by someone the victim knows, such as a classmate or boyfriend. In fact, one study showed that eight out of ten sexual assault victims know their attackers.

Sometimes, attackers use date rape drugs to sedate, impair, or even incapacitate their victims before their assault. The drug Rohypnol, also known as "roofies," has no taste, color, or smell. It can be slipped into a victim's drink without his or her knowledge. Roofies are illegal in the United States.

assault might not be serious enough to take to the police. Other times, they worry that reporting to the police will make their assault public knowledge. Sexual crimes that are reported to the police can be punished criminally.

A study of nearly three dozen colleges and universities from 2011 to 2013 shows how differently these institutions reprimanded students accused of sexual assault. In approximately 30 percent of cases, schools expelled students who were found guilty of sexual assault. Approximately 47 percent of the time, the students were suspended.[5] Many schools look to the Association for Student Conduct Administration (ASCA) for guidance on how to treat student misbehavior. The ASCA recommends schools take an educational rather than punitive approach to handling misconduct. In other words, they hope schools can teach students to behave better rather than punish them. Being expelled from school is regarded as a serious punishment. Some schools have interpreted this stance as a recommendation to keep accused students on campus as part of their reform. Critics of this practice argue that while this may benefit the accused, it often leaves the accuser feeling vulnerable and unsupported by the school.

In 2013, a woman was sexually assaulted in her Harvard dorm, or house. After pressuring administrators to have the man moved to another house, the victim wrote a public letter to the university. In it, she revealed that she had developed depression, insomnia, and terrible stress as a result of her assault. She also outlined how she had worked to convince the school to move the man. She argued that she did everything she could to have the man punished:

> Dear Harvard: I am writing to you to let you know that I give up. I will be moving out of my House next semester, if only— quite literally—to save my life. . . . My assailant will remain unpunished, and life on this campus will continue its course as if nothing had happened. Today, Harvard, I am writing to let you know that you have won.[6]

FROM THE
HEADLINES

BROCK TURNER

Late one night in 2015, two Stanford University graduate students were biking home. The cyclists noticed a man named Brock Turner acting strangely behind a dumpster. As they approached, they saw that Turner was sexually assaulting a half-naked, unconscious woman. Turner saw the cyclists and attempted to flee. The cyclists tackled him and called the police. Turner, a Stanford swimmer, was arrested and charged with five counts of sexual assault, including rape of an unconscious person.

Turner claimed that the sexual encounter was consensual. His lawyers said that he had only fled the cyclists because he was sick. Turner wrote a letter to the judge in which he said his actions had been influenced by a "party culture" of "binge drinking and sexual promiscuity." In her own statement, the victim argued Turner was missing the point: "Campus drinking culture. That's what we're speaking out against? . . . Not awareness about campus sexual assault, or rape, or learning to recognize consent."

Turner's swimming career was discussed at length during the trial. His lawyers argued that punishing him would surely ruin his swimming career. The victim responded to this in her statement: "How fast Brock swims does not lessen the severity of what

Demonstrators protested the relatively light sentence that Turner received, calling for the removal of the judge involved.

happened to me, and should not lessen the severity of his punishment."[7] Turner faced a maximum sentence of 14 years in jail. In the end he was sentenced to six months in jail and three years of probation. USA Swimming, the organization that governs American competitive swimming, banned Turner for life.

A MATTRESS PROTEST AND PERFORMANCE

In 2012, Columbia University student Emma Sulkowicz alleged she was raped by fellow student Paul Nungesser. Sulkowicz filed a complaint with the university, but Columbia cleared Nungesser of responsibility. The school agreed with Nungesser that the encounter was consensual.

Sulkowicz turned her anger and frustration into a performance art piece called Carry That Weight. This involved carrying a mattress—resembling the one on which she says she was raped—everywhere she went on campus. Carry That Weight was a protest against Columbia and a show of solidarity with victims of sexual assault. Sulkowicz even carried her mattress across the stage as she graduated.

Nungesser maintained his innocence, and he also felt that the performance was an example of bullying. He said that the performance art piece made it hard for him to get an education.

RECOGNIZING RAPE CULTURE AT SCHOOL

Many colleges and universities are working to fight campus sexual assault. One way they are doing this is by increasing student education about the issue. Some schools are requiring incoming and returning students to take classes about healthy relationships, alcohol and drug use, date rape, and how to report sexual violence.

Many institutions are focusing on the issue of consent. At California universities, students must receive affirmative consent before engaging in sexual acts. This means that a student must say "yes." This has often been called the "yes means yes" law. It challenges the old idea that a person must say "no" to show that he or she is not interested in a sexual encounter. Now, a person must unambiguously say "yes" to give consent. Schools in the rest of the country have followed California in adopting similar policies.

Some campuses are hoping that bystander intervention training will reduce the number of sexual assaults. This teaches students to intervene if they see a potentially risky situation. These programs often ask students to imagine they are at a party and role-play different scenarios. Bystander intervention training acknowledges that friends and even strangers can help prevent sexual violence.

Some students have encouraged schools to openly acknowledge rape culture. Anna Voremberg, the managing director of End Rape on Campus, says schools need to define rape culture for their students in their sexual assault policies. She says it "helps to have parameters for the

STUDENT ACTIVISM

Many college students have mobilized to fight campus sexual assault. Organizations such as Students Active for Ending Rape (SAFER) work to reform campus sexual assault policies. End Rape on Campus (EROC) is an activist group dedicated to helping survivors and preventing further sexual violence through campus education and policy reform. In 2014, President Obama commended the activism he had seen around the country.

conversation you're having on campus, so defining rape culture is important."[8]

Few schools have used the words *rape culture* in their policies. In part this is because the term is so controversial that some administrators feel it takes away from the content of the policies. For example, when Carleton University in Canada used the term in a preliminary draft of its sexual assault policy, a community debate erupted.

New York governor Andrew Cuomo signed a bill in 2015 that would require New York colleges and universities to have affirmative-consent policies.

Many felt the term was misguided. They felt discussing rape culture took away from the attention that should be paid to individuals. Some felt using the term made the school look as though it had a rape problem, when they argued it did not. After months of debate and controversy, the school decided to keep the term.

While few doubt rape occurs on campus, the extent to which it occurs and the ways it is handled by media, police, and school administrations remain controversial. People who claim rape culture is a social problem look to campus rape as one of its most obvious symptoms. Others see campus rape as the criminal behavior of troubled individuals. Peggy Orenstein, the author of *Girls and Sex: Navigating the Complicated New Landscape*, believes simply discussing campus rape can be a powerful step in making it less common: "The key may be to keep the bright light of public attention shining" on college campuses.[9]

CHAPTER SEVEN

THE LEGAL
SYSTEM

N avigating the legal system can be intimidating. This can be especially true for people involved in sexual assault litigation. Both the accuser and the accused are often faced with the daunting task of untangling a complex web of legal terms. They also face the steep costs of hiring lawyers. The legal system involves many of the central issues discussed within the rape culture debate, such as victim blaming, rape excusing, and the debate over the way rapes are reported and criminalized. Rape survivor Amanda Nguyen remembers struggling to pursue justice after her assault: "The system tells survivors to go to authorities to get help. I did that, but navigating the broken system was worse than the rape itself."[1]

The complex and stressful nature of the legal process can deter victims from seeking justice.

DIFFERING LAWS AND DEFINITIONS

LEGAL COMPLEXITY AND UNDERREPORTING

Some people argue that the complexity of rape laws contributes to an environment in which rape victims do not report their assaults. One survey found that 35 percent of sexual assault victims did not report their experiences because it was "unclear that it was a crime or that harm was intended."[2]

Many people point to these statistics as unreliable. *Washington Post* writer Michelle Ye Hee Lee reminds readers that "estimating the rate of cases that were *not reported* is always going to be just that—an estimate."[3] She urges caution when seeing such statistics.

The United States does not have one consistent set of laws governing rape. Rather, each state has its own set of rules. Some states do not even use the word *rape*. They use phrases such as *criminal sexual conduct* or *sexual abuse* instead.

States also differ in the ways they discuss consent. Some states require a victim to say "no," while others accept silence as a lack of consent. Some states are pursuing affirmative-consent laws that mirror California's university system's, in which a "yes" is required from both parties in a sexual interaction.

North Carolina law states that rape has not occurred if a victim consents to sex at one point and then changes his or her mind later during the sexual act. For example, in 2010, a teenage girl in Charlotte supposedly consented to sex with a football player, but then asked him to stop when it hurt. The football player persisted. The girl later accused him of rape, saying she had never consented in the first place. Her accusations were dismissed after the court referred to the state law that says if sexual interaction begins consensually, "no rape has occurred though the victim later withdraws consent during the same act of intercourse."[4]

If a victim is incapacitated because of drugs or alcohol, she or he is not able to consent. Many state laws handle a perpetrator's knowledge of a victim's incapacitation differently. Some do not clarify this subject at all.

RAPE AND ABORTION

Abortion remains a hotly debated topic in American politics. Some feel the question of whether to remain pregnant is a woman's personal decision. Others believe abortion should be criminalized. Many fall on a spectrum between the two. Many point to rape or incest as reasons why abortion should be allowed. They feel that a woman should not have to carry a child conceived under these circumstances.

DOES RAPE LAW CONTRIBUTE TO RAPE CULTURE?

Some critics argue that the wide range of rape laws, and the subtleties within each state's legal definition of rape,

BILL COSBY AND THE STATUTE OF LIMITATIONS

Each state has different statutes of limitations for crimes such as rape. These are legal expiration dates. An accusation must be leveled before the expiration date in order to pursue criminal charges. Many states have a statute of limitations of 10 years for sexual assault. Pennsylvania's is 12 years.

In the 2000s, comedian Bill Cosby was accused by dozens of women of sexually assaulting them. As these accusations were reported by the media, more women came forward. In the end, more than 50 women accused Cosby of sexual assault. This wave of accusations highlighted the importance of statutes of limitations. Some of the accusations related to incidents dating as far back as 1965. This meant that they were too old to pursue in criminal court.

In 2015, a woman named Andrea Constand filed criminal charges against Cosby. She accused him of drugging and sexually assaulting her in Pennsylvania in 2004. Her accusation fell within the statute of limitations. This meant Cosby could be criminally charged for the first time.

have contributed to rape culture. Writer Clare Kelly says, "By telling a victim his or her assault was not *legally* assault, we take the blame away from the victim's perpetrator and place it solely on the victim's shoulders." Kelly also points to the way some states have not updated their rape laws as problematic: "Whenever an outdated statute causes a rapist to walk free, society is *excusing* rape."[5]

Some people do not feel that the laws surrounding rape reinforce rape culture. Rather, they believe that the laws have evolved to help maintain social order, protect people, and punish offenders. They are satisfied that the laws adequately punish those convicted of rape. *Bloomberg* writer Megan McArdle acknowledges that rape is "a terrible crime," but cautions that people should not let the emotions that accompany rape affect the way it is handled in the judicial system. She urges her readers to "treat rape like every other crime" and assume that the accused is indeed innocent until proven guilty.[6]

SURVIVORS AND THE LAW

Today, many survivors of sexual assault are working to update and improve rape laws and advocate for victims. Nguyen has turned her assault into motivation to help others. She started Rise, a group that advocates for legal protections for people who have survived sexual assault. Rise pushed for the Sexual Assault Survivors' Rights Act, a measure President Obama signed into law in 2016. This law guarantees victims of sexual assault the right to a free rape kit, among other protections. A rape kit is the name commonly used for a forensic exam in which medical professionals can collect DNA evidence and provide medical care. Rape kits give survivors the chance to store

evidence against their attackers if they decide to pursue legal action against them.

Many local rape-victim advocacy groups exist to help survivors of sexual assault navigate the complex laws in each state. These groups can assist survivors in finding lawyers, provide educational materials, and give emotional support.

UNTESTED RAPE KITS

Today, experts estimate there is a backlog of hundreds of thousands of untested rape kits in the United States. This means the DNA evidence collected has not been analyzed. Some suggest that this can happen when prosecutors or detectives do not request a DNA analysis for each kit. Others think this is because many analysis labs in charge of the rape kits are not required to complete the DNA analysis under any clear timelines. Historically, few legal jurisdictions had well-defined systems for tracking or counting their rape kits. Today, states are working to address this issue by keeping better track of their rape kits and working to test as many as possible.

Obama spoke out forcefully during his presidency about laws designed to counter sexual assault.

FROM THE
HEADLINES

#FREEKESHA

In 2014, musician Kesha filed a civil suit against her music producer, Dr. Luke. The suit alleged that Dr. Luke had drugged and sexually and emotionally abused Kesha over the course of her music career. Kesha wanted to break her contract with Dr. Luke so she could continue to create music away from his influence. The suit claimed that in some instances, Dr. Luke had "forced himself" on the musician when she had been "intoxicated and drugged."[7] Dr. Luke soon filed a lawsuit against Kesha. This suit claimed that Kesha's accusations were false and were an attempt to bully Dr. Luke into releasing her from her contract.

Over a series of legal battles, many of Kesha's claims have been either rejected by the court or withdrawn. The expensive process has taken a toll on the musician. She attributes this to Dr. Luke's desire to punish her for her accusations. She said, "Dr. Luke promised me he would stall my career if I ever stood up for myself for any reason. . . . He is doing just that."[8]

While many fans have banded around Kesha, using hashtags such as #FreeKesha to draw attention to her cause, not everyone sides with her. Dr. Luke's lawyer believes Kesha is lying. She says, "just because someone says it doesn't make it true."[9]

Fans and activists banded together to
support Kesha.

A CONTENTIOUS
FUTURE

Today, the term *rape culture* remains just as controversial as ever. While crowds of marchers gather to protest rape culture on college campuses or participate in SlutWalks across the country, critics remain on the sidelines, skeptical of the impact or even the existence of rape culture. Many doubt that cultural attitudes surrounding sex can influence people enough to turn them into rapists or assaulters. Further, some critics wonder if the focus on rape culture is harmful not only to the falsely accused but also to society itself.

Many anti-rape activists emphasize that the responsibility to prevent rapes lies with rapists, not victims.

TITLE IX

Some of the current debate over rape culture and sexual assault law in the United States revolves around a law that dates back to 1972. Title IX is a law that has guaranteed gender equality in federally funded schools for more than 40 years. The law covers a broad range of things, such as career education and math and science education. One of the most well-known components of Title IX relates to school sports. It ensures that female and male students have equal access to sporting activities.

Title IX is an important component of the rape culture discussion because it states that schools are obliged to address and prevent any type of sexual harassment that makes it hard for students to learn. In 2011 and 2014, the Obama administration doubled down on its efforts

GRAY RAPE

In 2007, the magazine *Cosmopolitan* defined *gray rape* as "sex that falls somewhere between consent and denial and is even more confusing than date rape because often both parties are unsure of who wanted what."[1]

Some have welcomed this term, appreciating its nuance. They propose that "gray rape" can invite conversation about the complexities of sexual encounters, especially those that occur under the influence of alcohol. Others disagree. Neil Irvin, director of community education at Men Can Stop Rape, says, "rape is still rape."[2]

to enforce this part of Title IX. The Office for Civil Rights (OCR), an agency within the US Department of Education that works to ensure equal opportunities for all students in federally funded schools, got involved. It investigates schools to make sure they handle cases of sexual violence appropriately and with enough rigor. By 2016, the OCR was investigating more than 300 schools.

The crackdown under the Obama administration sent the message that schools must be aggressive in fighting campus sexual harassment. Not everyone thought this was good. Some schools criticized the push as being overzealous and leading to too many innocent students being punished for crimes they did not commit. For example, in 2015, a group of Wesley College fraternity men filmed a sexual encounter between a man and a woman. The woman was not aware she was being filmed. The school expelled the men within a week of the incident. One of the men maintained that he was innocent. The woman on the film also said that he was not involved. The school did not interview any of the men it expelled. The student who claimed that he was not involved tried to appeal to the school, but his attempt was blocked. In

Activist Dr. Bernice Sandler played a key role in creating Title IX.

the end, the Department of Education found that Wesley's swift response had violated the accused students' rights.

In 2014, a group of Harvard professors wrote an open letter criticizing the aggressive stance schools such as Harvard were taking to prevent sexual violence. They felt that the procedures designed to investigate and try allegations of sexual misconduct "lack[ed] the most basic elements of fairness and due process" and "are overwhelmingly stacked against the accused."[3] Elizabeth Bartholet, a professor at Harvard Law School, also found fault with the new, aggressive interpretation of Title IX. She said, "I believe that history will demonstrate the federal government's position to be wrong, that our society will look back on this time as a moment of madness."[4]

Early in his presidency, Donald Trump withdrew an Obama-era Title IX protection for transgender students. Some have wondered if he will also interpret the law differently regarding campus sexual harassment. Trump has said in the past that the Department of Education itself was not needed, leading some to wonder if Trump will turn over the responsibility for all sexual harassment and assault to the criminal-justice system. This could affect the way rape is discussed, punished, and prevented on college campuses and elsewhere.

A NEW WAY TO DISCUSS RAPE AND RAPE CULTURE

Today, the way rape and rape culture are discussed is evolving. Many experts are recommending that parents start talking to their children about consent long before they reach puberty. This involves teaching kids to respect their peers and also to accept rejection. Learning that "no means no" as children, these experts hope, could help these kids retain that notion when they become sexually active adults.

Some activists are encouraging rape survivors to talk more about their experiences in order to confront and battle rape culture. *XO Jane* writer and rape survivor Emily, who does not provide her last name, says, "I will publicly and

FIGHTING RAPE-SPLAINING

In 2013, *Ms.* magazine coined a new term: *rape-splaining.* Writer Natasha Turner proposed this new term to describe various attempts "to explain away cases of rape and assault." She went on to list ten examples, including "the victim was asking for it," or "the victim didn't say no."[5]

In 2014, R&B singer CeeLo Green was accused of rape-splaining on Twitter after he tweeted, "if someone is passed out they're not even WITH you consciously, so WITH implies consent" and "Women who have really been raped REMEMBER!!!" Green had been accused of date raping a woman in 2012. His tweets were related to the court case following these accusations, in which he pleaded no contest to drugging the woman without her knowledge. Green soon deleted the tweets, apologized, and stated he would "never condone the harm of any women."[6]

clearly state my experiences for all the people who can't or won't, because every time I do, I know I help someone understand what happened to them. And because every time I show my face and say the word, it takes the darkness and shame off me, the victim, and puts it squarely back where it belongs—on the perpetrators."[7]

This movement toward talking more about rape has been empowering for some but troubling for others. Some academic institutions are utilizing "trigger warning" policies before discussing potentially disturbing topics, such as rape or sexual assault. These warnings are designed to protect students from encountering material or discussions that might trigger trauma. For example, Aishah Shahidah Simmons, who teaches at Temple University, tells students on the first day of class that "we are getting ready to delve into some really difficult, painful information here."[8] Still, she worries about the concept of trigger warnings interfering with free speech, and she avoids using the phrase *trigger warning*. Some have pointed to this shift as a positive acknowledgment of the prevalence of rape and rape culture. Others disagree. They think trigger warnings coddle students, stifle free speech,

Aishah Shahidah Simmons, herself a victim of rape, uses trigger warnings in the courses she teaches at Temple University in Pennsylvania.

and stunt emotional growth. In 2016, the University of Chicago released a letter to incoming students in which it declared that the school did not support the idea of trigger warnings: "We do not condone the creation of intellectual 'safe spaces' where individuals can retreat from ideas and perspectives at odds with their own."[9]

While the discussion about rape culture continues to shift in tone and content, one thing is certain: more and more people are talking about rape. Rape features prominently in popular movies, novels, television shows, and music. Male and female celebrities have come forward to discuss their own rapes. As rape continues to saturate popular culture and educational institutions, some wonder whether this attention will contribute to higher rates of rape and sexual assault or whether greater awareness will help prevent these crimes. Some have even suggested that the focus on sexual assault awareness could actually help would-be perpetrators learn how to commit sexual assault without getting caught.

THE SHIFTING ROLE OF RAPE JOKES

Critics often point to rape jokes as both symptoms of and causes of rape culture. When people joke about rape, they reduce its social and psychological impact. Joking about it can also normalize it. Comedian and actor Seth Rogen's work has put him at the center of several rape-joke controversies. His 2009 comedy *Observe and Report* featured a scene in which two characters have sex while the woman is passed out. His 2016 animated film *Sausage Party* showed a character forcing another into a suggestive act while insisting, "if you say anything, no one will believe you." Many have criticized Rogen for making light of rape. Sexual assault survivor Morgana LeBold wrote why his *Sausage Party* joke bothered her: "the more we add [sexual assault] to movies for comedic effect, the more we lose."[10]

Not everyone agrees that rape jokes are a problem. Some feel that they can be a powerful part of the conversation about rape and rape culture. Comedian Sarah Silverman has used rape jokes to raise awareness. In 2015, she tweeted a list of rape-prevention tips, including "If you are in an elevator and a woman gets in, don't rape her" and "Carry a rape whistle. If you find that you are about to rape someone, blow the whistle until someone comes to stop you."[11] This tweet has been praised for bringing attention to rape and sparking conversations about the roles of victims and perpetrators in rape culture.

A CALL TO ACTION

Rape and sexual assault are crimes that can cause terrible physical and mental strain on their victims. Whether they are a symptom of rape culture, simply the behaviors of individuals, or some combination of the two is something society continues to debate.

What is not up for debate, however, is the fact that more work needs to be done to reduce the rate of sexual violence in the United States. In 2014, Vice President Joe Biden urged Americans to take action: "Our daughters, our

Silverman often pushes boundaries in her comedy, discussing rape and other taboo topics.

MORE TO THE
STORY

MEN AS PART OF RAPE CULTURE

One controversial element of rape culture is the idea that the male gender in general is responsible for the rampant sexual violence committed against women. Many people reject this, claiming that it paints men with too broad a brush. Others urge men to consider the idea.

Writer Zaron Burnett III says: "If you are a man, you are part of rape culture. I know . . . that sounds rough. You're not a rapist, necessarily. But you do perpetuate the attitudes and behaviors commonly referred to as rape culture." Burnett goes on to clarify his point, telling his readers that "men commit 99 percent of rapes," and that even if a man hasn't committed a rape himself, his actions almost certainly contribute to the environment in which rape is normalized.

Burnett acknowledges that this is an unfair burden men must bear: "You didn't create it. But you also didn't build the freeways either. Some of the things you inherit from society are cool and some of them are rape culture."[12]

sisters, our wives, our mothers, our grandmothers have every single right to expect to be free from violence and sexual abuse." He continued, "No matter what she's wearing, no matter whether she's in a bar, in a dormitory, in the back seat of a car, on a street, drunk or sober—no man has a right to go beyond the word 'no.'"[13] Many others have echoed his sentiment, expanding it to include other genders.

Today, academics, law enforcement officers, parents, lawyers, counselors, celebrities, and activists are working to heed Biden's call. They are striving for a future in which rape and sexual assault are less common and in which survivors receive more support.

TEACHING KIDS ABOUT BODILY BOUNDARIES

Some parents hope to raise children who will not engage in or promote rape culture. A 2016 *Huffington Post* article titled "How to Prevent a Brock," referring to Brock Turner, listed different ways parents could fight rape culture.

One of the tips focused on teaching kids about healthy bodily boundaries. It emphasized that children should learn that their own bodily boundaries should be respected, and that they must always respect the boundaries of others. This means parents should not force their children to hug or kiss family members if they don't want to and that tickling games must always stop when the child says "stop." The article explains that this is the "kid version of 'no means no.'"[14] Learning this at a young age might encourage children to remain respectful of other people's bodily boundaries into adulthood.

ESSENTIAL
FACTS

MAJOR EVENTS

- The documentary film *Rape Culture* is released in 1975, drawing attention to the prevalence and acceptance of rape and other forms of sexual violence.

- On August 11, 2012, two Steubenville High School football players are recorded sexually assaulting an intoxicated 16-year-old girl. In 2013, both are found guilty of rape.

- In 2015, Brock Turner is seen sexually assaulting an unconscious woman. In 2016, Turner is sentenced to six months in jail and three years of probation.

KEY PLAYERS

- Caroline Kitchens has written several influential articles denouncing rape culture as a harmful and misleading concept based on flawed research.

- Amanda Nguyen was raped in 2013. After her assault, she created Rise, a nonprofit organization that fights for rape survivors' rights.

- President Barack Obama was an outspoken advocate for victims of sexual assault and worked to adopt new legislation to protect them during his two terms in office.

IMPACT ON SOCIETY

- Rape and other forms of sexual assault have an unquestionably negative impact on society. These actions hurt victims and their families. They can lead to lengthy, expensive, and emotionally difficult legal battles. Sometimes, victims feel as though they are not respected or listened to. Other times, victims remain silent about their assaults and suffer alone. People who have been falsely accused of rape suffer as well. They often struggle to repair their reputations.

- The notion of rape culture, though controversial, has led to discussions about how best to prevent and investigate incidents of sexual assault. It has also spurred conversations about how best to punish those found guilty of sexual assault. Some maintain that rape culture is alive and well and is one of the causes for the high numbers of rapes and sexual assaults in America. Others find this claim dubious. They believe that rape and sexual assault are the actions of individuals, and nothing more.

QUOTE

"Nearly one in five women in America has been a victim of rape or attempted rape. . . . It's not okay. And it has to stop."

—President Barack Obama, 2015

GLOSSARY

ACQUITTED
Found not guilty of a criminal act.

ALLEGE
To claim or assert.

BROTHEL
A building in which prostitutes work.

CONSENT
To agree or give permission for something to happen.

DNA
Deoxyribonucleic acid, the chemical that is the basis of genetics, through which various traits are passed from parent to child.

EPIDEMIC

The widespread occurrence of something negative.

HACKTIVISTS

People who carry out computer hacking in order to achieve social justice or a political cause.

HATE CRIME

A crime motivated by prejudice against the victim.

LITIGATION

The process of taking legal action.

SEX-POSITIVE

Promoting a tolerant or progressive attitude toward sexuality.

STATUTORY RAPE

Sexual intercourse with a minor.

ADDITIONAL
RESOURCES

SELECTED BIBLIOGRAPHY

Cohen, Sascha. "How a Book Changed the Way We Talk about Rape." *Time*. Time, 7 Oct. 2015. Web. 31 Mar. 2017.

"Sexual Violence." *CDC*. CDC, 2012. Web. 18 Mar. 2017.

Sinozich, Sofi. "Rape and Sexual Assault Victimization among College-Age Females, 1995–2013." *BJS*. Bureau of Justice Statistics, December 2014. Web. 4 Apr. 2017.

FURTHER READING

Berlatsky, Noah. *Sexual Violence*. Farmington Hills, MI: Greenhaven, 2014.

Ghafoerkhan, Olivia. *Sexual Assault: The Ultimate Teen Guide*. Lanham, MD: Rowman & Littlefield, 2017.

Harding, Kate. *Asking for It: The Alarming Rise of Rape Culture—and What We Can Do about It*. Boston, MA: Da Capo, 2015.

ONLINE RESOURCES

Booklinks
NONFICTION NETWORK
FREE! ONLINE NONFICTION RESOURCES

To learn more about rape culture and sexual violence, visit **abdobooklinks.com**. These links are routinely monitored and updated to provide the most current information available.

MORE INFORMATION

For more information on this subject, contact or visit the following organizations:

National Sexual Violence Resource Center (NSVRC)
2101 N. Front Street
Governor's Plaza North, Building #2
Harrisburg, PA 17110
717-909-0710
nsvrc.org
This organization works to prevent sexual violence and improve the way sexual-violence response works. NSVRC works to collaborate with health-care workers, researchers, advocates, and more to educate the public about sexual violence and its prevention.

Rape, Abuse & Incest National Network (RAINN)
202-544-1034
rainn.org
RAINN is the largest anti-sexual violence organization in the United States. It partners with more than 1,000 sexual assault support providers around the country.

SOURCE
NOTES

CHAPTER 1. A SUMMER PARTY IN OHIO

1. Maia Szalavitz. "What about the Victim: The Steubenville Rape Victim's Recovery." *Time*. Time, 20 Mar. 2013. Web. 12 July 2017.

2. Conor Friedersdorf. "The Understudied Female Sexual Predator." *Atlantic*. Atlantic Monthly, 28 Nov. 2016. Web. 12 July 2017.

3. "Frequently Asked Questions about the Change in the UCR Definition of Rape." *Uniform Crime Reporting*. FBI, 11 Dec. 2014. Web. 12 July 2017.

4. Adam Clark Estes. "CNN's Not the Only One Peddling Sympathy for the Steubenville Rapists." *Atlantic*. Atlantic Monthly, 17 Mar. 2013. Web. 12 July 2017.

5. "Victims of Sexual Violence." *RAINN*. RAINN, 2016. Web. 12 July 2017.

6. "Statistics About Sexual Violence." *NSVRC*. NSVRC, 2015. Web. 12 July 2017.

7. "Sexual Violence: Facts at a Glance." *CDC*. CDC, 2012. Web. 12 July 2017.

8. Libby Nelson. "The Future of Obama's Sweeping Fight against Sexual Assault Now Lies with Donald Trump." *Vox*. Vox Media, 23 Nov. 2016. Web. 12 July 2017.

CHAPTER 2. THE EVOLVING HISTORY OF RAPE CULTURE

1. Sarah Deer. "Toward an Indigenous Jurisprudence of Rape." *Faculty Scholarship*. Mitchell Hamline Open Access, 2004. Web. 12 July 2017.

2. Jessica Hopper. "Rosa Parks' Letter Release Detailing Rape Attempt Angers Her Institute." *ABC News*. ABC News, 3 Aug. 2011. Web. 12 July 2017.

3. Laura Beck. "These Vintage Pants Give Us the Creeps." *Jezebel*. Jezebel, 6 Mar. 2013. Web. 12 July 2017.

4. Sascha Cohen. "How a Book Changed the Way We Talk about Rape." *Time*. Time, 7 Oct. 2015. Web. 12 July 2017.

5. "Child Sexual Abuse Statistics." *Victims of Crime*. National Center for Victims of Crime, 2012. Web. 12 July 2017.

6. Caroline Kitchens. "It's Time to End Rape Culture Hysteria." *Time*. Time, 20 Mar. 2014. Web. 12 July 2017.

7. Barbara Kay. "'Rape Culture' Fanatics Don't Know What a Culture Is." *National Post*. National Post, 8 Mar. 2014. Web. 12 July 2017.

8. "Sexual Assault and the LGBT Community." *HRC*. HRC, 2017. Web. 12 July 2017.

9. Caroline Kitchens. "It's Time to End Rape Culture Hysteria." *Time*. Time, 20 Mar. 2014. Web. 12 July 2017.

10. Caroline Kitchens. "The Rape 'Epidemic' Doesn't Actually Exist." *US News*. US News and World Report, 24 Oct. 2013. Web. 12 July 2017.

CHAPTER 3. SLUT SHAMING AND VICTIM BLAMING

1. Jessica Valenti. "Rape Is Not Inevitable: On Zerlina Maxwell, Men and Hope." *Nation*. Nation, 12 Mar. 2013. Web. 12 July 2017.

2. Megan Gibson. "Study: Women Slut-Shame Each Other on Twitter as Much as Men Do." *Time*. Time, 21 May 2014. Web. 12 July 2017.

3. Jessica Valenti. "In Rape Tragedies, the Shame Is Ours." *Nation*. Nation, 17 Apr. 2013. Web. 12 July 2017.

4. Emily Lindin. "If You've Ever Ordered Pizza, Then You Already Understand What Consent Is." *Teen Vogue*. Condé Nast Digital, 27 Apr. 2016. Web. 12 July 2017.

5. Amber Jamieson. "Derrick Rose Rape Accuser's Name to Be Made Public." *Guardian*. Guardian News, 21 Sep. 2016. Web. 12 July 2017.

6. Lauren Barbato. "This Anti-Slut Shaming Rule in Derrick Rose's Case Has a Major Flaw." *Bustle*. Bustle, 28 Sep. 2016. Web. 12 July 2017.

CHAPTER 4. THE MASCULINE IDEAL

1. Pamela Paresky. "What's Wrong with Locker Room Talk?" *Psychology Today*. Sussex Publishers, 10 Oct. 2016. Web. 12 July 2017.

2. Sarah Childress. "Why the Military Has a Sexual Assault Problem." *Frontline*. PBS, 10 May 2013. Web. 12 July 2017.

3. Nina Burleigh. "'He Grabbed Me': Woman Alleges Trump Groped Her Exactly as Described on Tape." *Newsweek*. Newsweek, 8 Oct. 2016. Web. 12 July 2017.

4. Allan Smith. "Palin Calls Trump Comments 'Disgusting.'" *Business Insider*. Business Insider, 8 Oct. 2016. Web. 12 July 2017.

5. Gloria Steinem. "Sexual Violence against Women Is the Result of the Cult of Masculinity." *Guardian*. Guardian News, 24 Feb. 2012. Web. 12 July 2017.

6. Michael Carter. "How to Be a Man: Redefining Masculinity." *Huffington Post*. Huffington Post, 2 May 2014. Web. 12 July 2017.

7. "Lesbian, Gay, Bi-Sexual, Transgendered (LGBT) Populations and Sexual Assault." *WCASA*. WCASA, 2013. Web. 12 July 2017.

CHAPTER 5. FALSE REPORTING

1. Dara Lind. "What We Know About False Rape Allegations." *Vox*. Vox Media, 1 June 2015. Web. 12 July 2017.

2. Jonathan Wells. "'Guilty until Proven Innocent': Life After a False Rape Accusation." *Telegraph*. Telegraph Media Group, 28 Oct. 2015. Web. 12 July 2017.

SOURCE NOTES
CONTINUED

3. Jeremy Diamond and Eugene Scott. "Trump Says He'll Sue Sexual Misconduct Accusers." *CNN: Politics*. CNN, 22 Oct. 2016. Web. 12 July 2017.

4. Daniella Silva. "Trump Accuser Summer Zervos Files Defamation Suit against President Elect." *NBC News*. NBC News, 17 Jan. 2017. Web. 12 July 2017.

5. C. MacKinnon. *Feminism Unmodified*. Cambridge, MA: Harvard, 1987. Print. 4.

6. Cathy Young. "Crying Rape." *Slate*. Slate, 18 Sep. 2014. Web. 12 July 2017.

CHAPTER 6. THE COLLEGE CAMPUS

1. Tyler Kingkade. "Texas Tech Frat Loses Charter Following 'No Means Yes, Yes Means Anal' Display." *Huffington Post*. HP, 9 Oct. 2014. Web. 12 July 2017.

2. Mary Bowerman et al. "Is 'College Experience' Synonymous with Rape Culture?" *USA Today*. USA Today, 26 Aug. 2016. Web. 12 July 2017.

3. Jessica Valenti. "Frat Brothers Rape 300% More." *Guardian*. Guardian News, 24 Sep. 2014. Web. 12 July 2017.

4. Alexandra Svokos. "How Our Obsession with Getting Laid in College Blurs the Lines of Sexual Assault." *Elite Daily*. Elite Daily, 2 Dec. 2016. Web. 12 July 2017.

5. Tyler Kingkade. "Fewer Than One-Third of Campus Sexual Assault Cases Result in Expulsion." *Huffington Post*. HP, 29 Sep. 2014. Web. 12 July 2017.

6. "Dear Harvard: You Win." *Crimson*. Harvard, 31 Mar. 2014. Web. 12 July 2017.

7. Katie J. M. Baker. "Here Is the Powerful Letter the Stanford Victim Read Aloud to Her Attacker." *BuzzFeed News*. BuzzFeed, 3 June 2016. Web. 12 July 2017.

8. Jake New. "Defining Rape Culture." *IHE*. IHE, 7 Nov. 2016. Web. 12 July 2017.

9. Peggy Orenstein. *Girls and Sex*. New York: Harper Collins, 2016. Print.

CHAPTER 7. THE LEGAL SYSTEM

1. Neesha Arter. "Navigating the Broken System Was Worse than the Rape Itself." *Women in the World*. New York Times, 4 Feb. 2016. Web. 12 July 2017.

2. Stephanie Auteri. "Was It Rape? The Problems with Varying Definitions for Sexual Assault." *Pacific Standard*. SJF, 27 Jan. 2016. Web. 12 July 2017.

3. Michelle Ye Hee Lee. "The Truth About a Viral Graphic on Rape Statistics." *Fact Checker*. Washington Post, 9 Dec. 2014. Web. 12 July 2017.

4. Tom Roussey. "Dropped Rape Charge against Football Player Prompts Questions." *WBTV*. Raycom Media, 2010. Web. 12 July 2017.

5. Clare Kelly. "How State Laws Perpetuate Rape Culture." *Odyssey*. Odyssey Media, 3 May 2016. Web. 12 July 2017.

6. Megan McArdle. "Treat Rape Like Every Other Crime." *BloombergView*. Bloomberg, 7 July 2016. Web. 12 July 2017.

7. A. J. Willingham. "In Depth: The Battle Between Kesha and Dr. Luke Was Years in the Making." *CNN: Entertainment*. CNN, 23 Mar. 2016. Web. 12 July 2017.

8. Joe Coscarelli. "Kesha Went to Court against Dr. Luke. Now the Tables Are Turned." *New York Times*. New York Times, 20 Oct. 2016. Web. 12 July 2017.

9. Ibid.

CHAPTER 8. A CONTENTIOUS FUTURE

1. Laura Sessions Stepp. "A New Kind of Date Rape." *Cosmopolitan*. Hearst Communications, 10 Sep. 2007. Web. 12 July 2017.

2. Sewell Chan. "Gray Rape: A New Form of Date Rape?" *New York Times*. New York Times, 15 Oct. 2007. Web. 12 July 2017.

3. Samuel R. Bagenstos. "What Went Wrong with Title IX?" *Washington Monthly*. Washington Monthly, Sep./Oct. 2015. Web. 12 July 2017.

4. Christina Hoff Sommers. "The Media Is Making College Rape Culture Worse." *Daily Beast*. Daily Beast Media, 23 Jan. 2015. Web. 12 July 2017.

5. Natasha Turner. "Rape-Splaining: 10 Examples of Victim Blaming." *Ms. Magazine*. Ms. Magazine, 28 May 2013. Web. 12 July 2017.

6. Colin Stutz. "CeeLo Green Tweets 'Women Who Have Really Been Raped Remember.'" *Billboard*. Billboard, 1 Sept. 2014. Web. 12 July 2017.

7. "Why I Talk about Rape." *xo Jane*. Time, 25 Jan. 2012. Web. 12 July 2017.

8. Maria Flynn. "The Trouble with Trigger Warnings." *Huffington Post*. Huffington Post, 22 Dec. 2016. Web. 12 July 2017.

9. Elizabeth Chuck. "University of Chicago: We Don't Condone Safe Spaces or 'Trigger Warnings.'" *NBC News*. NBC News, 26 Aug. 2016. Web. 12 July 2017.

10. Morgana LeBold. "Why the Rape Scene in Sausage Party Wasn't Funny." *Huffington Post*. HP, 16 Aug. 2016. Web. 12 July 2017.

11. Stacey Cole. "Sarah Silverman Almost Died Last Week, and Why She Still Tells Rape Jokes." *Inquisitr*. Inquisitr, 14 July 2016. Web. 12 July 2017.

12. Zaron Burnett III. "A Gentleman's Guide to Rape Culture." *Human Parts*. Medium, 29 May 2014. Web. 12 July 2017.

13. Jackie Calmes. "Obama Seeks to Raise Awareness of Rape on Campus." *New York Times*. New York Times, 22 Jan. 2014. Web. 12 July 2017.

14. Em & Lo. "How to Prevent a Brock: 10 Practical Ways Parents Can Fight Rape Culture." *Huffington Post*. Huffington Post, 17 June 2016. Web. 12 July 2017.

INDEX

ABOUT THE
AUTHOR

Rebecca Rissman is an award-winning children's author. Her writing has been praised by *School Library Journal*, *Booklist*, *Creative Child Magazine*, and *Learning Magazine*. She has written more than 300 books about history, science, art, and culture. Rissman is especially interested in American history, with an emphasis on the military, the police, and the government. She has also written titles about slavery, the black power movement, and Rodney King and the Los Angeles riots. Rissman lives in Chicago, Illinois, with her husband and two daughters.